ARTIST
TRANSCRIPTIONS
TRUMPET

Miles Davis Originals Vol. 2

Transcribed by Timo Shanko

Cover Photo: Raymond Ross

ISBN 0-634-00558-8

HAL•LEONARD®
CORPORATION
7777 W. BLUEMOUND RD. P.O. BOX 13819 MILWAUKEE, WI 53213

Visit Hal Leonard Online at
www.halleonard.com

Miles Davis Originals Vol. 2

Contents

Biography

Miles Davis was one of the most important musicians in American music. An individual trumpet stylist, Miles Davis had more career highs than six giants of the music scene combined. He left many landmark recordings in a career that spanned bebop, cool jazz, modal jazz, fusion and hip-hop. He also promoted and discovered some of the most important musicians in the jazz world, including Bill Evans, John Coltrane, Red Garland, Chick Corea, Dave Liebman, Ron Carter, Wayne Shorter, and many, many others.

Miles Dewey Davis was born on May 25, 1926 in Alton, Illinois, but grew up in East St. Louis. He began playing trumpet when he was nine or ten. He went to New York in 1944 to study at the Juilliard School of Music, but he really wanted to be part of the jazz scene, so he dropped out after a few months. He played with Coleman Hawkins on recordings and gigs on 52nd Street, but by 1945 Miles was playing and recording with Charlie Parker. His style at that time was often tentative, but Parker and other musicians believed in him. Miles later gained valuable experience in the Benny Carter Orchestra on the West Coast, but he was back with Parker by 1948.

Miles took over a nine-piece rehearsal band with arrangements by Gerry Mulligan, Gil Evans, George Russell, John Lewis, and John Carisi in late 1948. It played one or two live gigs with varying personnel, but became famous as the "Birth of the Cool" ensemble based on twelve recordings for the Capitol label. These recordings highlighted a new approach to ensemble jazz and improvisation and continue to be influential.

Miles worked infrequently in the early '50s mainly due to a substance abuse problem, but he kicked the habit by 1954. An appearance at the Newport Jazz Festival in 1955 was a major success for him, and during this period he led a quintet featuring John Coltrane, Red Garland, Paul Chambers and Philly Joe Jones. Along with albums with this lineup which are now considered jazz classics, he began an association with composer/arranger Gil Evans that yielded several large orchestral albums garnering spectacular reviews and influencing players and composers worldwide.

In 1959, with an all-star ensemble of Coltrane, Chambers, Cannonball Adderley, Bill Evans, and Jimmy Cobb, Miles recorded the album *Kind of Blue*. This album became one of the most consistent selling albums in the history of the recording industry; it continues to be a top-selling catalog recording. The music on the album kick-started the modal jazz movement, and two of the five tunes became jazz standards.

By 1964, Davis was leading another incredible ensemble which included tenor saxophonist Wayne Shorter, keyboardist Herbie Hancock, bassist Ron Carter, and drummer Tony Williams. While still playing standard songs and new compositions, the group was looser and incorporated more modern and even avant-garde elements. The music continued to evolve, and by 1968, Davis encouraged the musicians to incorporate electronics and rock. Soon Chick Corea, bassist Dave Holland and drummer Jack DeJohnette were the featured players, and this ensemble was later known as one of the earliest "fusion" ensembles. In fact, the double album *Bitches Brew* is cited as the recording that launched the fusion era of jazz. Long-time fans were confounded and alienated, but Miles pressed on in his new direction; his groups often included more than one guitar and/or keyboard. Miles was now controversial, and his live appearances were more popular with rock audiences than jazz fans. Ill health sidelined Davis in 1975, and for all intents and purposes, he'd retired. But in 1981, he was back with a group incorporating funk and modern pop music. One of the last concerts he played was a Quincy Jones-produced re-visit to the Birth of the Cool repertoire at the Montreux jazz festival. Miles died on September 28, 1991 in Santa Monica, California.

Agitation

By Miles Davis

Fast

♩ = 330

*N.C. (Free harmony)

* *Played primarily on D minor*

(Hey!)

9

Sax Solo (Open)

Piano Solo (Open)

Trumpet

Slower

Fine

Country Son

By Miles Davis

Played primarily on E7

Played primarily on E7

All Blues

By Miles Davis

*Could be written in 6/8

Bitches Brew

By Miles Davis

Open Vamp

Trumpet

N.C. (D)

Eighty One

By Miles Davis and Ronald Carter

Four

By Miles Davis

Trumpet Break (Head in played by Sax only)
*N.C.

The form and changes are not played literally, only suggestively.

Filles de Kilimanjaro

By Miles Davis

Miles

By Miles Davis

* *Loose and interpretive with regard to chord changes and form.*

Open Sax Solo   Open Piano Solo   **B** **Head**
Bm

A D11

3

Tag

4

Fine

rit -

Miles Runs the Voodoo Down

By Miles Davis

Petits Machins

By Miles Davis and Gil Evans

Seven Steps to Heaven

By Miles Davis and Victor Feldman

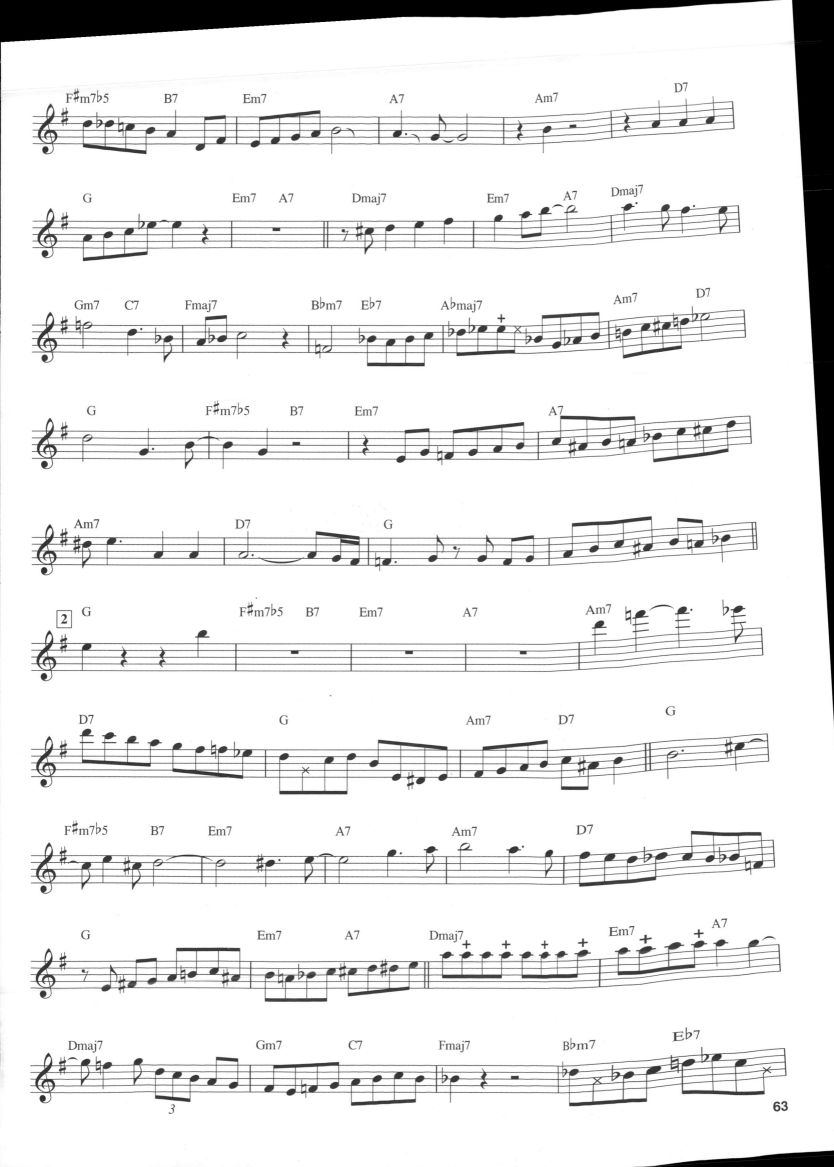

So What

By Miles Davis

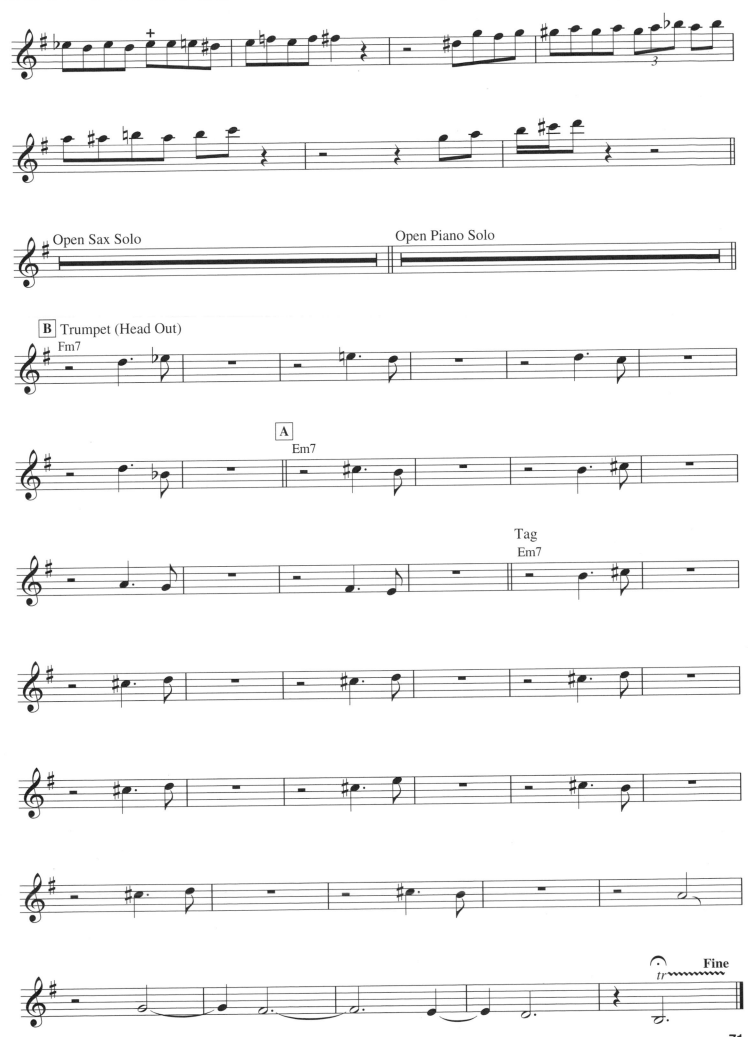

Spanish Key

By Miles Davis

Rhodes Solo/(B.S. Clar. Solo)

82

F#7

3

(B)

Fade   Fine

No Blues

By Miles Davis